Oxford Children's Picture Dictionary

L. A. Hill and Charles Innes

Illustrated by Barry Rowe

Oxford University Press

Oxford University Press, Walton Street, Oxford OX2 6DP

Oxford New York Toronto
Delhi Bombay Calcutta Madras Karachi
Petaling Jaya Singapore Hong Kong Tokyo
Nairobi Dar es Salaam Cape Town
Melbourne Auckland

and associated companies in
Berlin Ibadan

Oxford English and the *Oxford English logo* are
trade marks of Oxford University Press

ISBN 0 19 431260 7 (hardback)
ISBN 0 19 431240 2 (paperback)
© Oxford University Press 1981
Eighth impression 1989

Set in Monophoto Gill 262 by
BAS Printers Limited, Over Wallop, Hampshire

Printed in Hong Kong

Contents

1 into space

2 in the country

3 on the farm

4 in the town

5 in the supermarket

6 in the street

7 fruit and vegetables

8 in the park

9 in the classroom

10 the house . . .

11 . . . and garden

12 in the kitchen

13 at the table

14 the living-room

15 the hall

16 a bedroom at night

17 a bedroom in the day

18 the bathroom

19 making things

20 from the post office

21 at the birthday party

22 my body

23 my head

24 the family

25 clothes

26 at the fire

27 bad weather

28 holiday at the seaside

29 on the sea

30 in the sky

31 to the rescue

32 at the hospital

33 bad luck

34 sport

35 sport

36 sport

37 by road

38 at the zoo

39 large and small animals

40 music

41 helping

42 having fun

43 doing things

44 where are we?

45 where are they going?

46 pairs

47 pairs

48 what time is it?

49 what is the date?

50 colours

51 numbers

index

into space 1

1 rocket

2 space-shuttle

3 sun

4 astronaut

5 space-suit

6 moon

7 orbit

8 earth/world

9 satellite

10 planet

11 star

12 launch-pad

13 space-station

14 control-room

15 capsule

2 in the country

1 mountain

2 lake

3 valley

4 forest

5 hill

6 village

7 river

8 wood

9 field

10 farm

11 path

12 caravan

13 tent

14 stream

15 pond

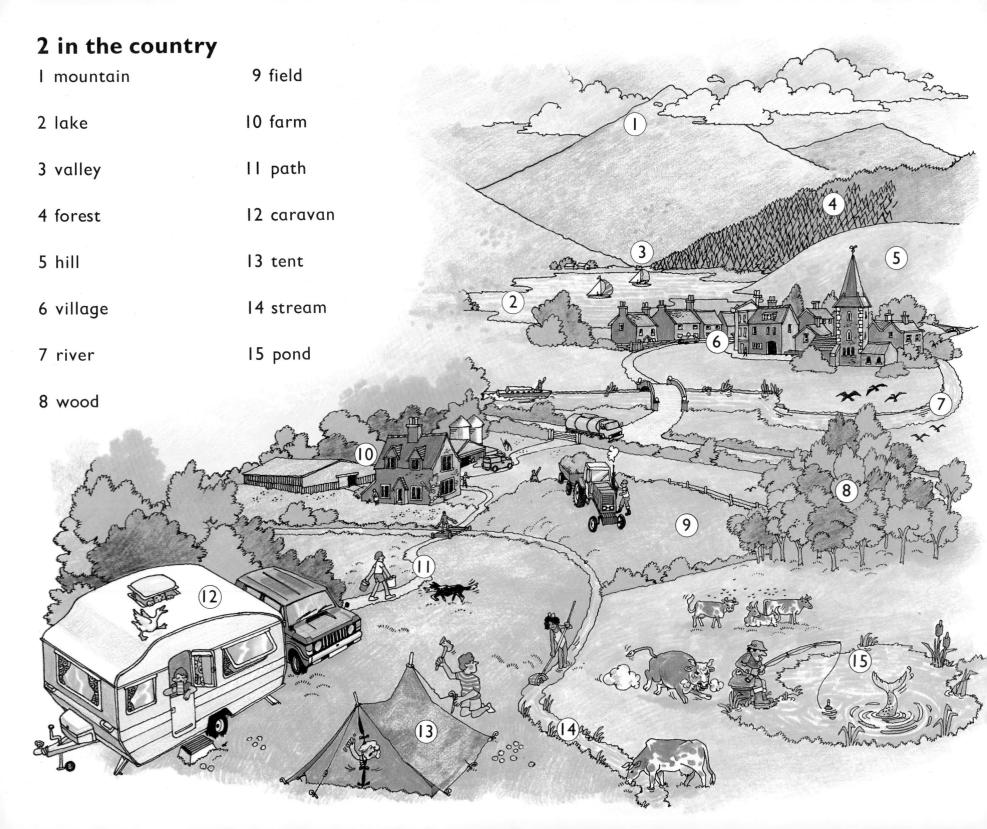

1 horse	6 sheep	11 cow
2 cart	7 goat	12 bird
3 donkey	8 fence	13 hedge
4 farmer	9 chicken	14 pig
5 tractor	10 rabbit	15 duck

4 in the town

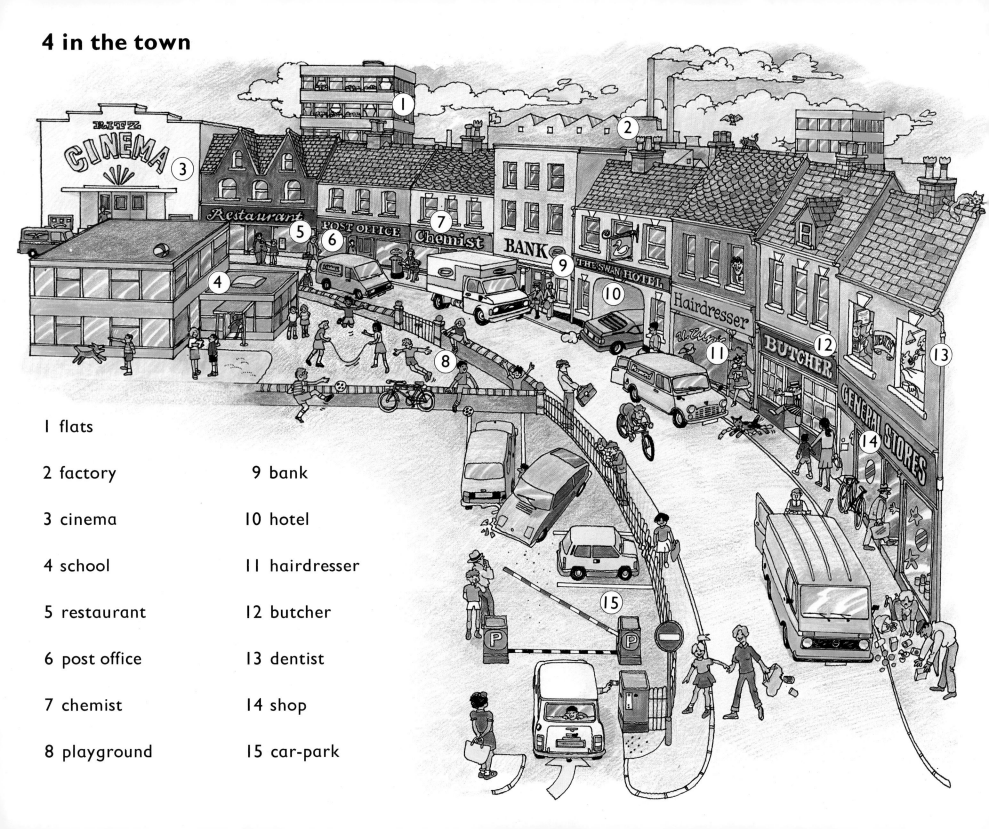

1 flats

2 factory

3 cinema

4 school

5 restaurant

6 post office

7 chemist

8 playground

9 bank

10 hotel

11 hairdresser

12 butcher

13 dentist

14 shop

15 car-park

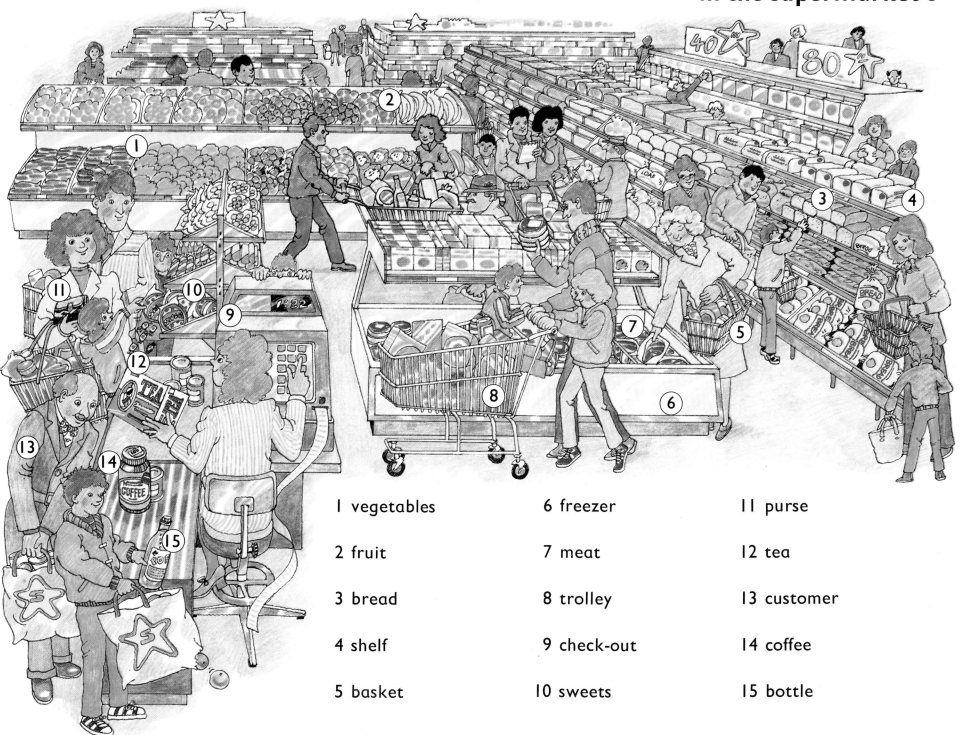

1 vegetables	6 freezer	11 purse
2 fruit	7 meat	12 tea
3 bread	8 trolley	13 customer
4 shelf	9 check-out	14 coffee
5 basket	10 sweets	15 bottle

6 in the street

1 police-station

2 corner

3 lorry

4 petrol-station

5 petrol-pump

6 lamp-post

7 telephone-box

8 bus-stop

9 road

10 bus

11 (pedestrian) crossing

12 traffic-light

13 crossroads

14 van

15 pavement

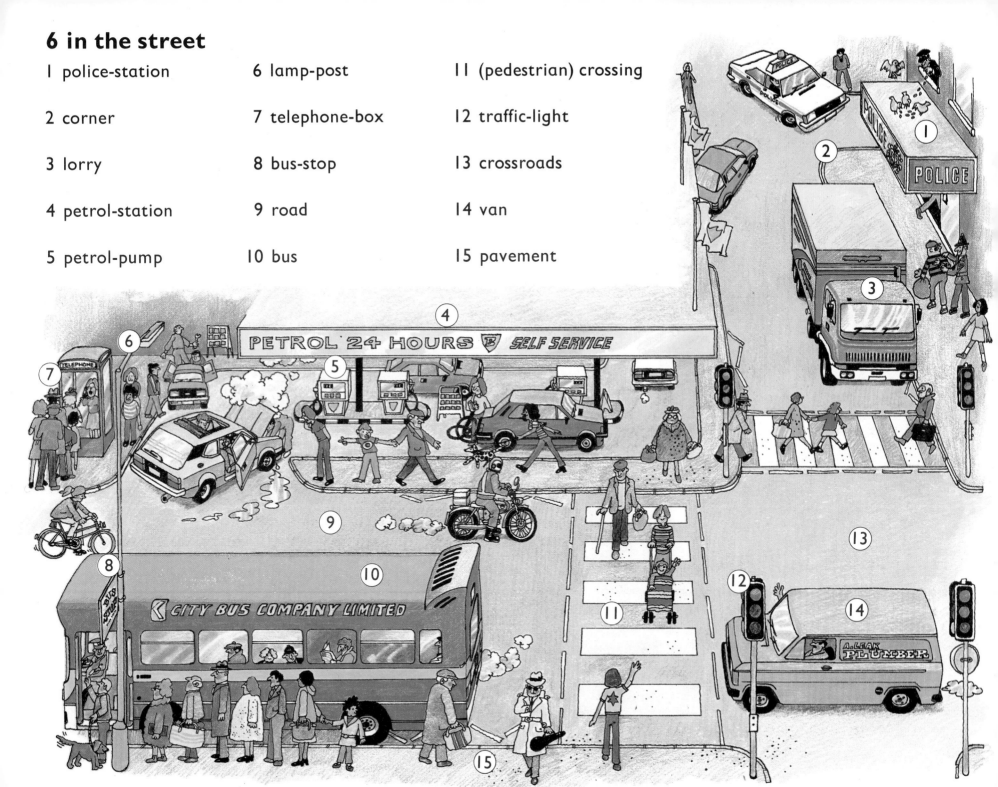

1 apples

2 pears

3 grapes

4 bananas

5 pineapple

6 oranges

7 lemons

8 lettuces

9 cabbages

10 cucumbers

11 beans

12 carrots

13 potatoes

14 onions

15 nuts

8 in the park

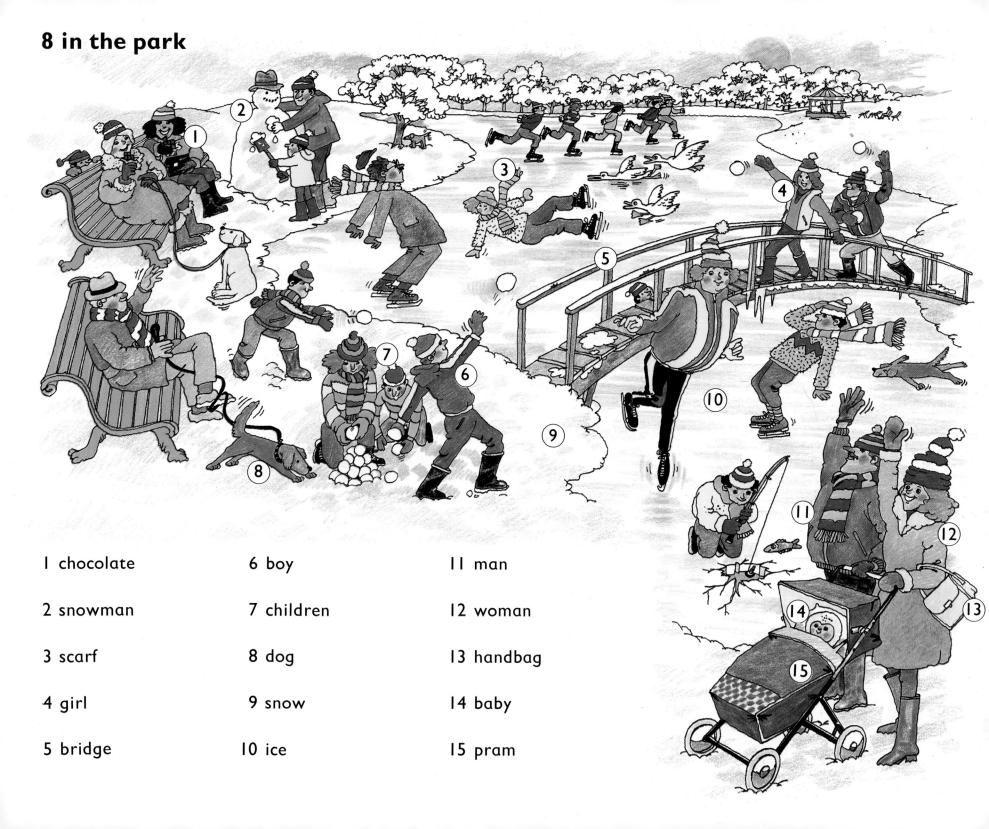

1 chocolate	6 boy	11 man
2 snowman	7 children	12 woman
3 scarf	8 dog	13 handbag
4 girl	9 snow	14 baby
5 bridge	10 ice	15 pram

in the classroom 9

1 map

2 teacher

3 chalk

4 blackboard

5 pupil

6 bookcase

7 book

8 desk

9 exercise-book

10 ruler

11 bag

12 rubber

13 pencil

14 pen

15 satchel

10 the house . . .

1 aerial

2 chimney

3 roof

4 upstairs

5 window

6 pipe

7 brick

8 downstairs

9 door

10 garage

11 dustbin

12 footpath

13 gate

14 washing-line

15 shed

1 tree

2 branch

3 leaf

4 (rope-)ladder

5 bush

6 swing

7 fence

8 see-saw

9 slide

10 grass

11 wheel-barrow

12 flower

13 (flower-)pot

14 fork

15 spade

12 in the kitchen

1 cooker	6 cheese	11 sink
2 grill	7 fridge	12 coffee-pot
3 oven	8 frying-pan	13 milk
4 washing-machine	9 pan	14 egg
5 can	10 kettle	15 (electric) mixer

at the table 13

1 mug

2 jug

3 fork

4 dining-table

5 plate

6 salt

7 pepper

8 spoon

9 bowl

10 knife

11 butter

12 jam

13 toast

14 glass

15 chair

14 the living-room

1 lamp

2 television

3 fireplace

4 (knitting-)needle

5 sofa

6 cushion

7 teapot

8 cup

9 saucer

10 tray

11 waste-paper basket

12 armchair

13 wool

14 stool

15 radio

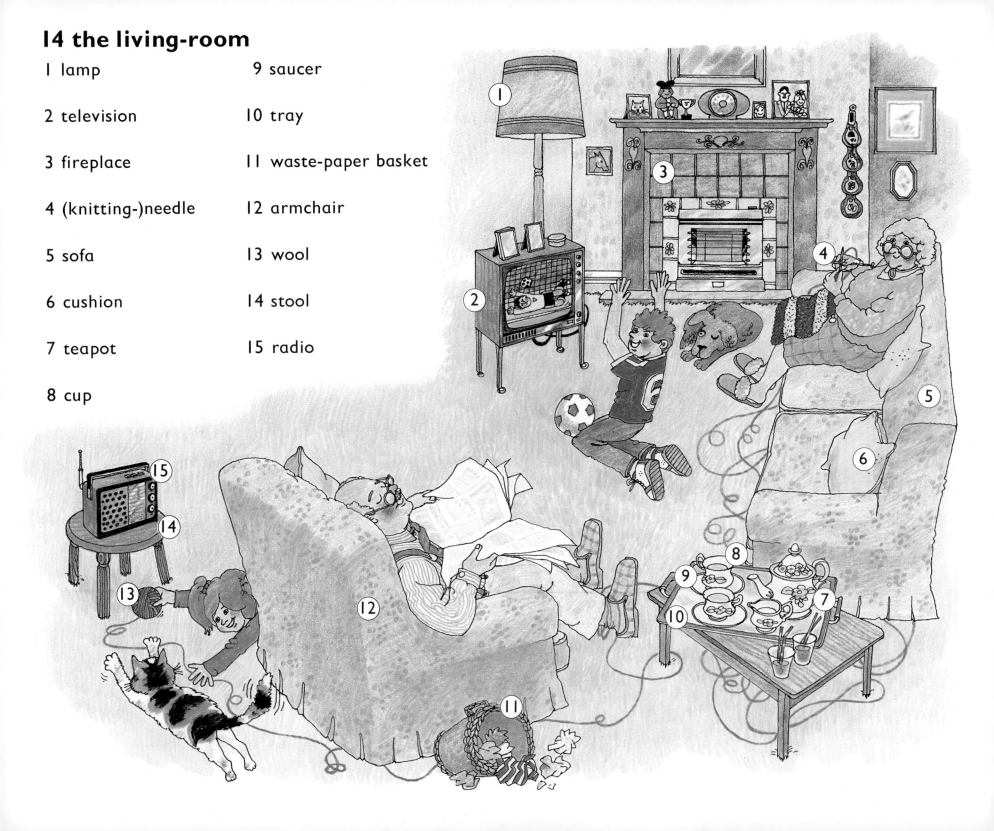

1 ceiling

2 wall

3 light

4 picture

5 (light-)switch

6 plant

7 telephone

8 staircase

9 cupboard

10 cardboard box

11 vacuum-cleaner

12 carpet

13 brush

14 dustpan

15 floor

16 a bedroom at night

1 dressing-gown

2 bed

3 nightie

4 blanket

5 sheet

6 pyjamas

7 pillow

8 curtain

9 (alarm-)clock

10 hairbrush

11 comb

12 slippers

13 rug

14 drawer

15 chest of drawers

1 poster

2 toys

3 castle

4 truck

5 carriage

6 platform

7 station

8 train

9 torch

10 brush

11 paints

12 paper

13 jigsaw

14 (board-)game

15 soldier

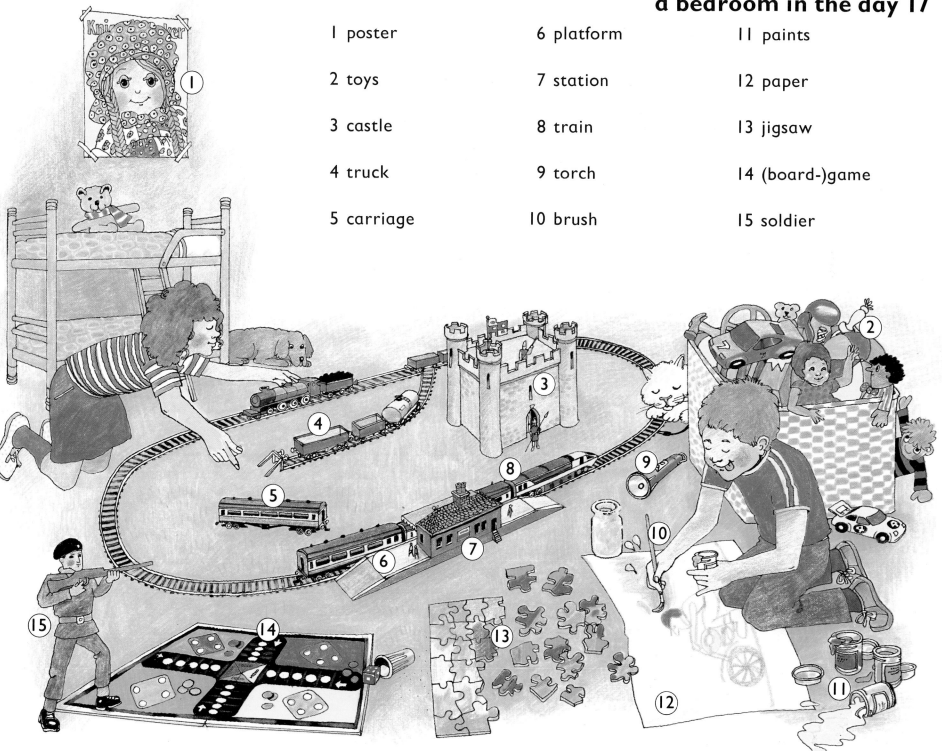

18 the bathroom

1 lavatory/toilet

2 lavatory-/toilet-paper

3 mirror

4 toothbrush

5 tap

6 toothpaste

7 basin

8 towel

9 scales

10 bathmat

11 shower

12 soap

13 shampoo

14 bath

15 sponge

1 iron

2 pin

3 sewing-machine

4 scissors

5 cotton

6 button

7 zip

8 doll's house

9 saw

10 penknife

11 glue

12 screw

13 screwdriver

14 nail

15 hammer

20 from the post office

1 letter

2 postman

3 string

4 postcard

5 parcel

6 letter-box/post-box

7 name

8 address

9 stamp

10 brake

11 pump

12 bicycle/bike

13 wheel

14 tyre

15 milk

1 friend

2 present

3 biscuit

4 camera

5 puppet

6 doll

7 game

8 balloon

9 ice-cream

10 candle

11 cake

12 slice

13 record

14 record-player

15 card

22 my body

1 hand

2 face

3 chest

4 tummy

5 finger

6 thumb

7 arm

8 head

9 elbow

10 back

11 bottom

12 knee

13 leg

14 foot

15 toe

1 chin

2 eyebrow

3 tongue

4 beard

5 mouth

6 hair

7 nose

8 moustache

9 ear-ring

10 eye

11 neck

12 cheek

13 lip

14 tooth

15 ear

24 the family

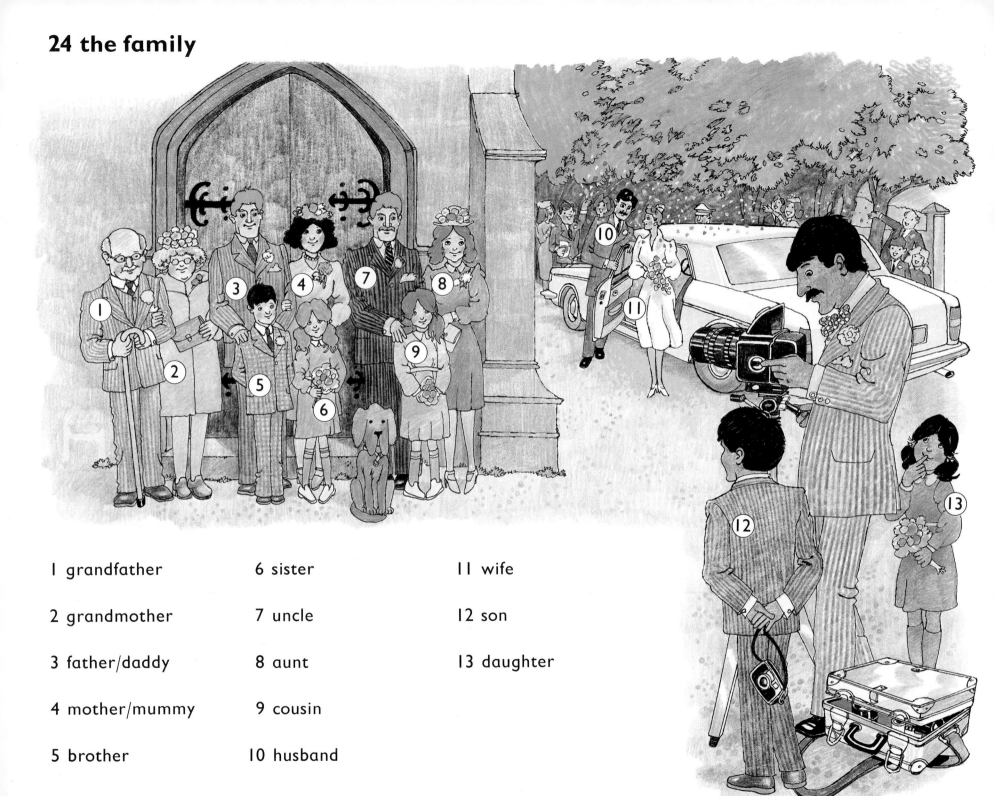

1 grandfather	6 sister	11 wife
2 grandmother	7 uncle	12 son
3 father/daddy	8 aunt	13 daughter
4 mother/mummy	9 cousin	
5 brother	10 husband	

1 T-shirt

2 trousers

3 sock

4 vest

5 pants

6 shorts

7 dress

8 sweater

9 jacket

10 jeans

11 pocket

12 skirt

13 shoelace

14 shoe

15 shirt

26 at the fire

1 fireman

2 smoke

3 ladder

4 fire-escape

5 fire

6 building

7 water

8 fire-engine

9 ambulance

10 crowd

11 police-car

12 policeman

13 (fire-)hose

14 axe

15 bell

1 rainbow

2 sky

3 cloud

4 lightning

5 rain

6 hat

7 wind

8 belt

9 coat

10 glove

11 cap

12 umbrella

13 raincoat

14 boot

15 puddle

28 holiday at the seaside

1 circus	6 picnic	11 swimming-costume
2 fair	7 net	12 swimming-trunks
3 canoe	8 ring	13 spade
4 shell	9 sun-glasses	14 bucket
5 drink	10 goggles	15 sand

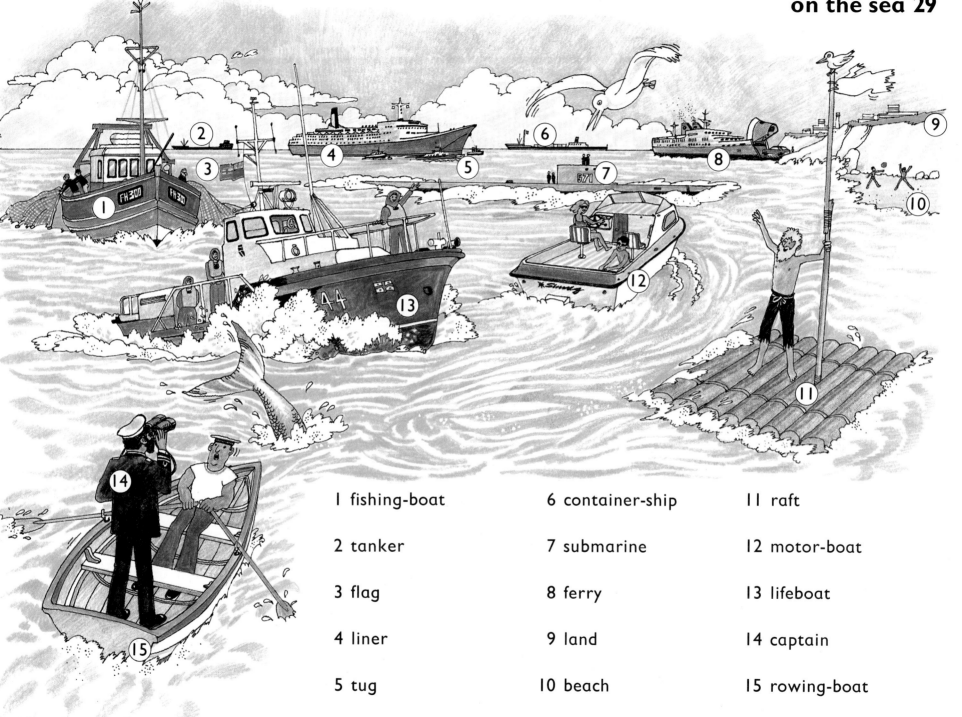

1 fishing-boat	6 container-ship	11 raft
2 tanker	7 submarine	12 motor-boat
3 flag	8 ferry	13 lifeboat
4 liner	9 land	14 captain
5 tug	10 beach	15 rowing-boat

30 in the sky

1 glider

2 balloon

3 parachute

4 kite

5 hotel

6 aeroplane

7 air hostess

8 airport

9 (jet) engine

10 wing

11 helicopter

12 runway

13 ticket

14 money

15 passenger

1 storm

2 helicopter

3 pilot

4 cliff

5 island

6 rope

7 sailor

8 ship

9 sail

10 sea

11 boat

12 wave

13 deck

14 hole

15 rock

32 at the hospital

1 lift

2 nurse

3 watch

4 handkerchief

5 glasses

6 doctor

7 injection

8 newspaper

9 photograph

10 patient

11 medicine

12 pills

13 bandage

14 stretcher

15 plaster

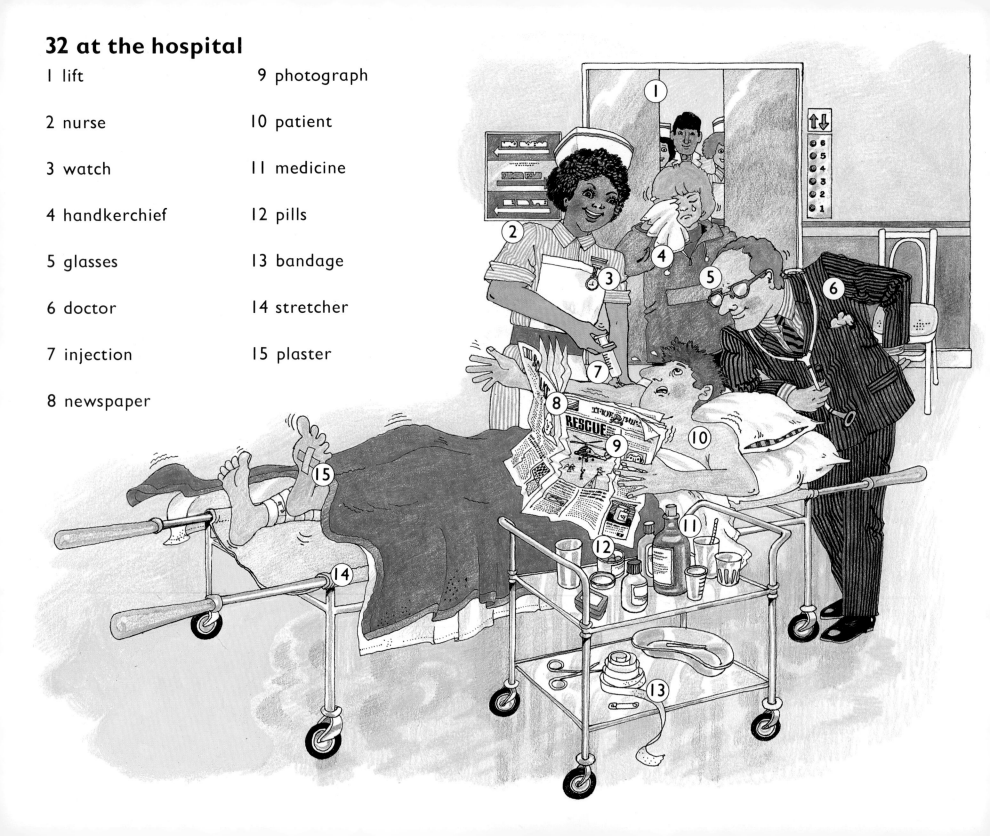

1 camp

2 break

3 fall

4 stand

5 carry

6 lie

7 pick up

8 cry

9 cut

10 bleed

11 write

12 sit

13 tear

14 tie

15 sting

34 sport

1 football	6 ball	11 basketball
2 goal	7 tennis	12 baseball
3 line	8 court	13 cricket
4 team	9 net	14 bat
5 player	10 racket	15 glove

1 skating

2 judo

3 cycling

4 swimming

5 swimming-pool

6 rugby

7 fishing

8 athletics

9 boxing

10 table tennis

11 motor-racing

12 ski-ing

13 rowing

14 trainers

15 track suit

36 sport

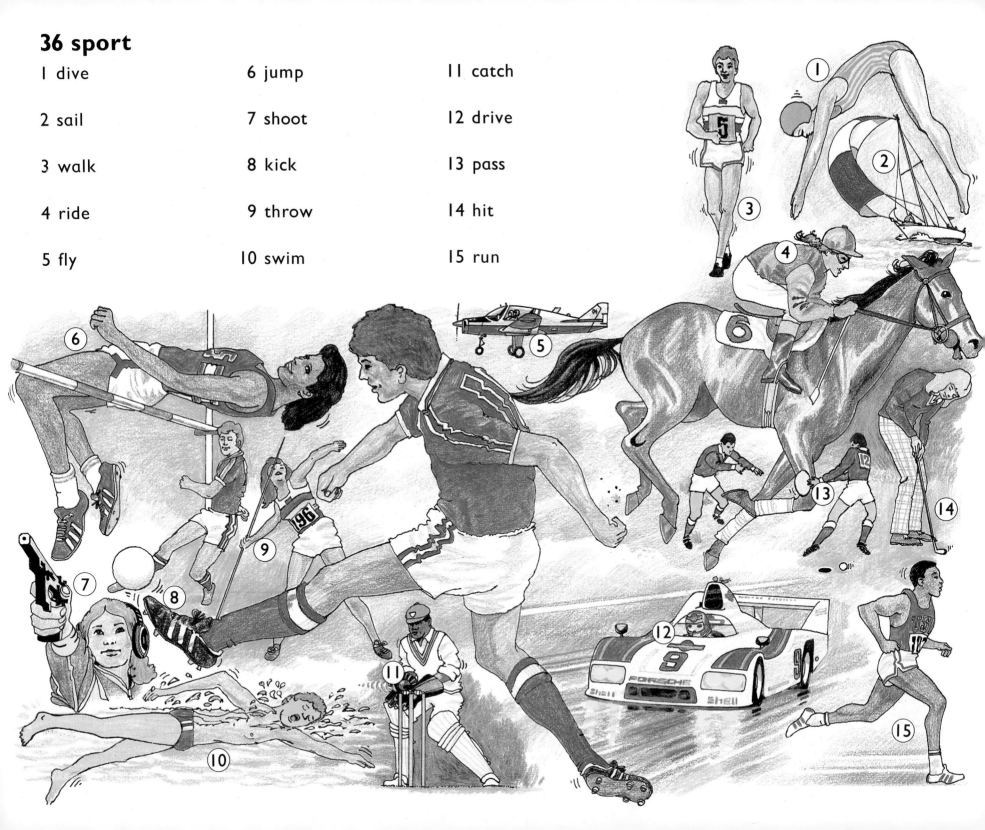

1 dive

2 sail

3 walk

4 ride

5 fly

6 jump

7 shoot

8 kick

9 throw

10 swim

11 catch

12 drive

13 pass

14 hit

15 run

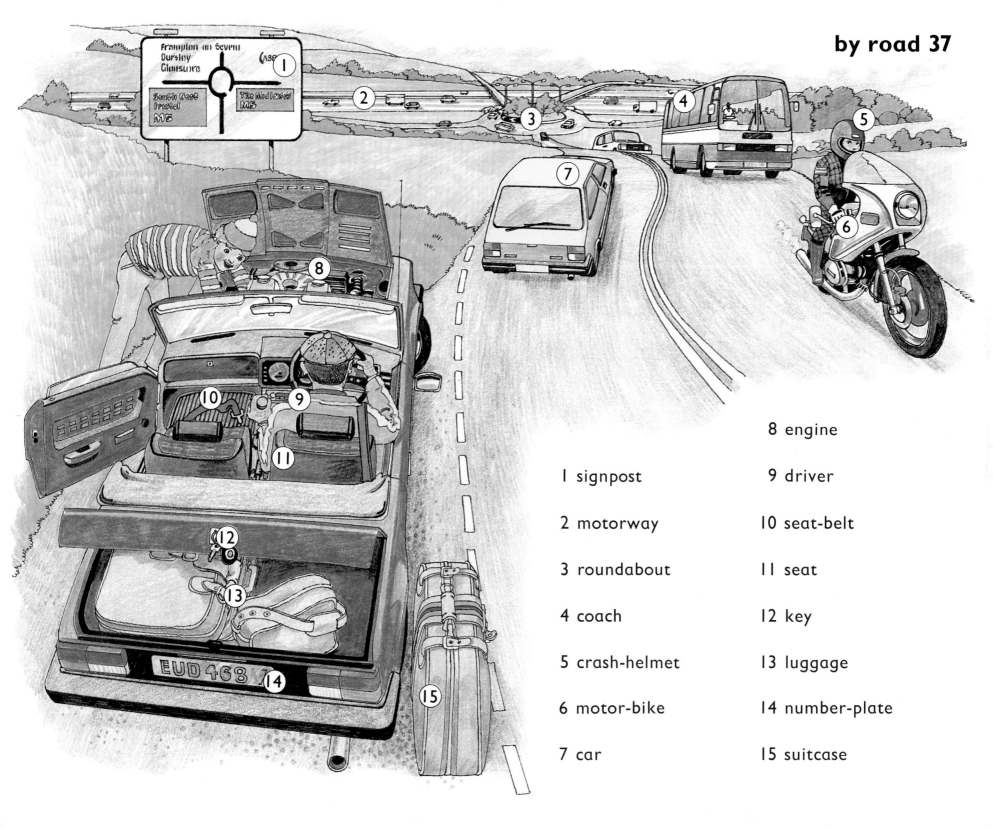

1 signpost

2 motorway

3 roundabout

4 coach

5 crash-helmet

6 motor-bike

7 car

8 engine

9 driver

10 seat-belt

11 seat

12 key

13 luggage

14 number-plate

15 suitcase

38 at the zoo

1 eagle

2 cage

3 tiger

4 crocodile

5 snake

6 lion

7 fish

8 dolphin

9 camel

10 bear

11 elephant

12 keeper

13 penguin

14 monkey

15 panda

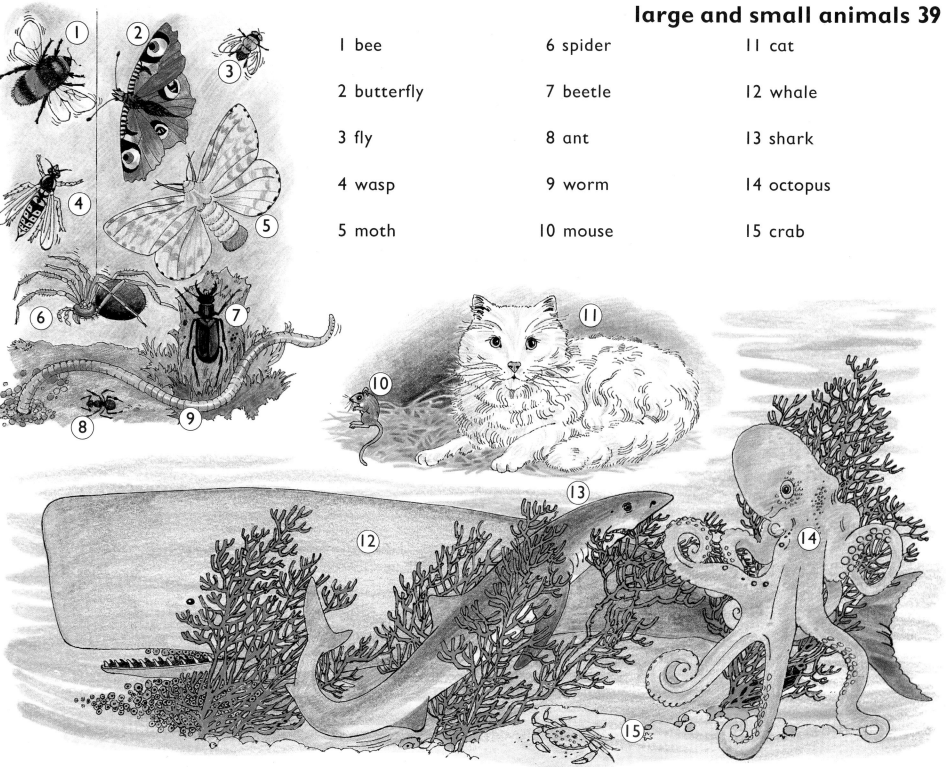

1 bee

2 butterfly

3 fly

4 wasp

5 moth

6 spider

7 beetle

8 ant

9 worm

10 mouse

11 cat

12 whale

13 shark

14 octopus

15 crab

40 music

1 trumpet

2 player

3 violin

4 recorder

5 drum

6 singer

7 (pop) group

8 microphone

9 string

10 piano

11 stool

12 guitar

13 cassette

14 music

15 record

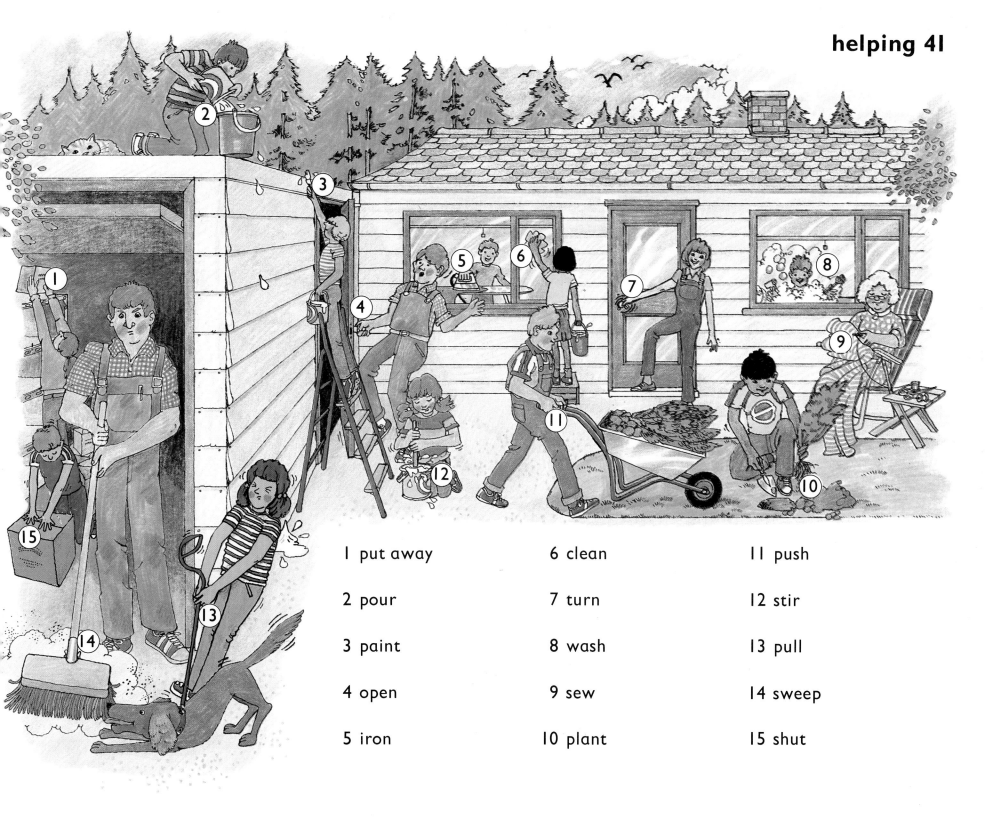

1 put away	6 clean	11 push
2 pour	7 turn	12 stir
3 paint	8 wash	13 pull
4 open	9 sew	14 sweep
5 iron	10 plant	15 shut

42 having fun

1 wave

2 kiss

3 laugh

4 swing

5 clap

6 shout

7 climb

8 shake (hands)

9 sing

10 play

11 dance

12 hug

13 give

14 smile

15 blow

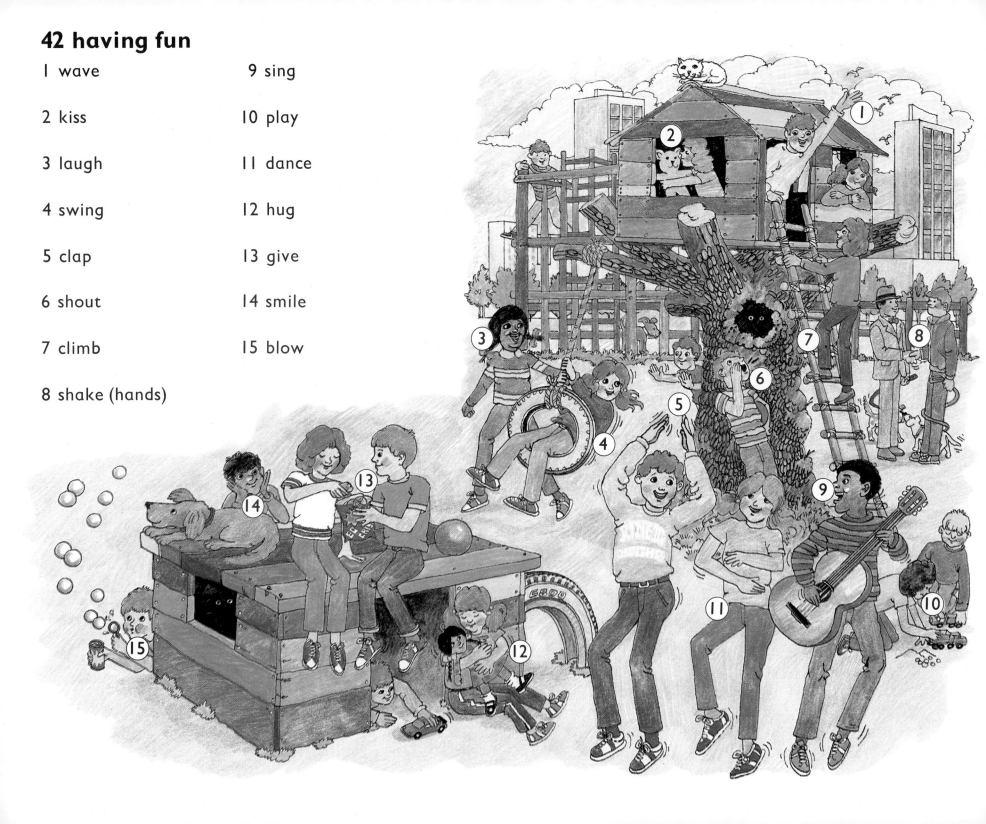

1 brush	6 eat
2 comb	7 drink
3 dream	8 bite
4 sleep	9 lick
5 wake	10 post

11 read
12 draw
13 listen
14 hide
15 crawl

44 where are we?

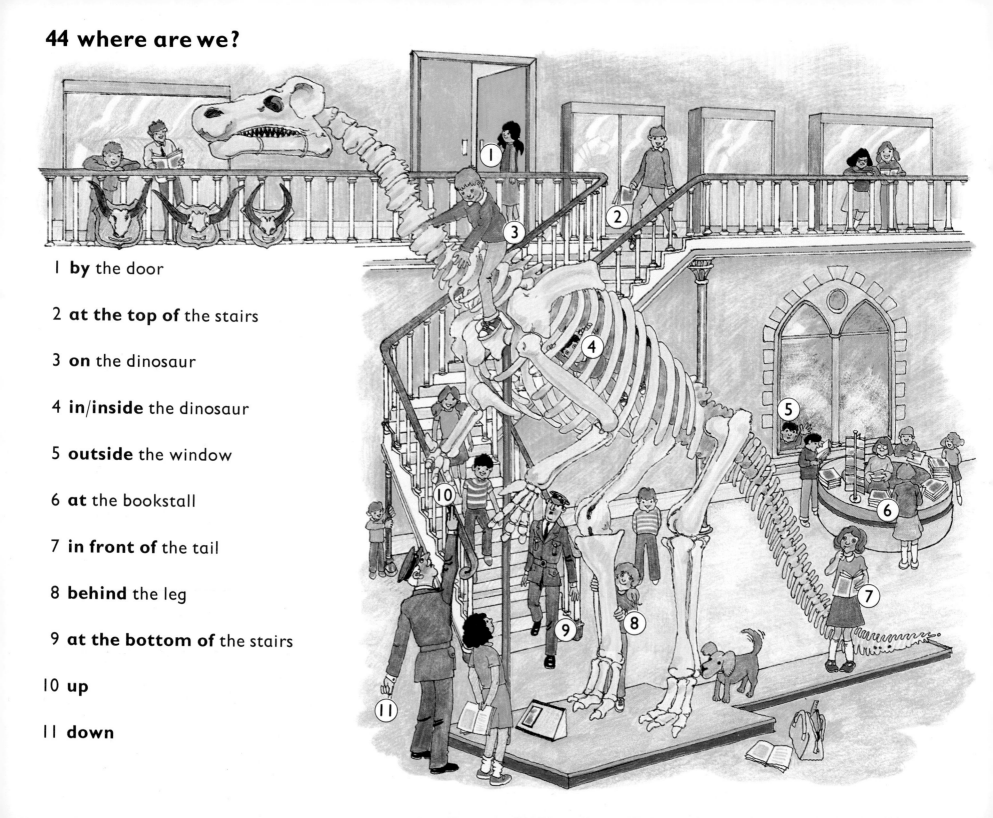

1 **by** the door

2 **at the top of** the stairs

3 **on** the dinosaur

4 **in/inside** the dinosaur

5 **outside** the window

6 **at** the bookstall

7 **in front of** the tail

8 **behind** the leg

9 **at the bottom of** the stairs

10 **up**

11 **down**

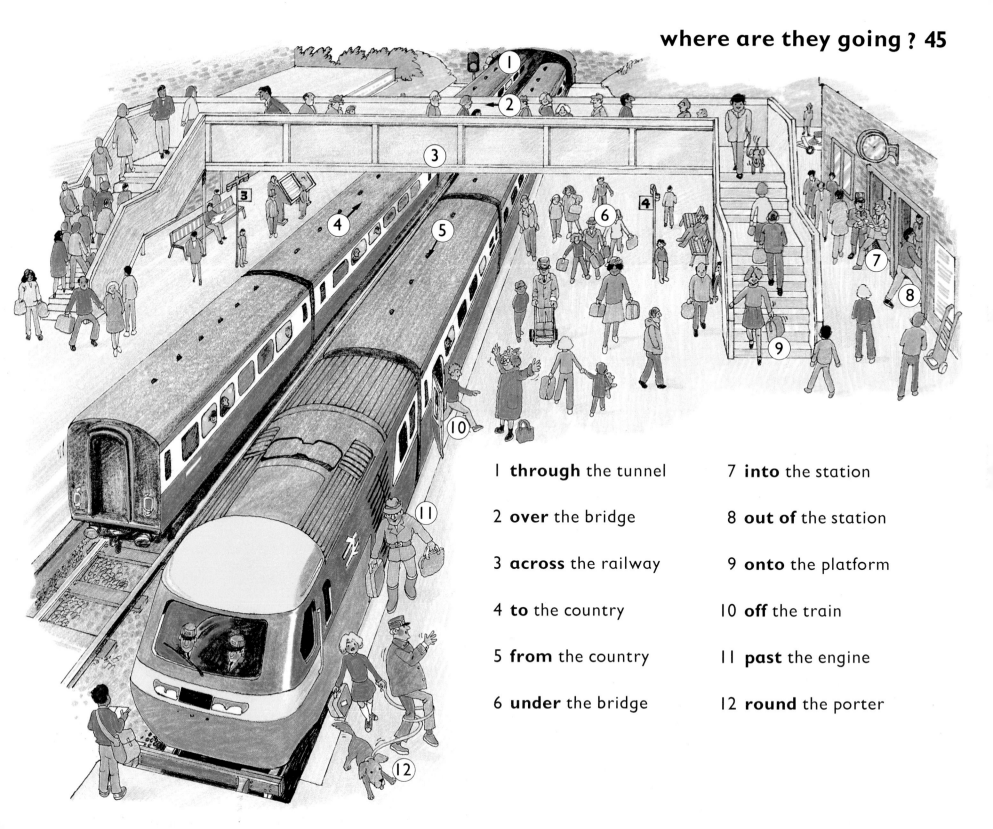

1 **through** the tunnel

2 **over** the bridge

3 **across** the railway

4 **to** the country

5 **from** the country

6 **under** the bridge

7 **into** the station

8 **out of** the station

9 **onto** the platform

10 **off** the train

11 **past** the engine

12 **round** the porter

46 pairs

beautiful   ugly   big   little   blunt   sharp

clean   dirty   easy   hard   empty   full

fast   slow   fat   thin

front   back   good   bad   happy   sad

heavy light	high low	hot cold
left right	dark light	short long
old new		open closed/shut
strong weak	wet dry	young old

48 what time is it?

five o'clock

half past four

quarter past six

quarter to three

60 seconds = 1 minute

60 minutes = 1 hour

24 hours = 1 day

7 days = 1 week

4 weeks = 1 month

12 months = 1 year

midnight

ten to seven

twenty past eight

noon

months

January

February

March

April

May

June

July

August

September

October

November

December

days of the week

Sunday

Monday

Tuesday

Wednesday

Thursday

Friday

Saturday

50 colours

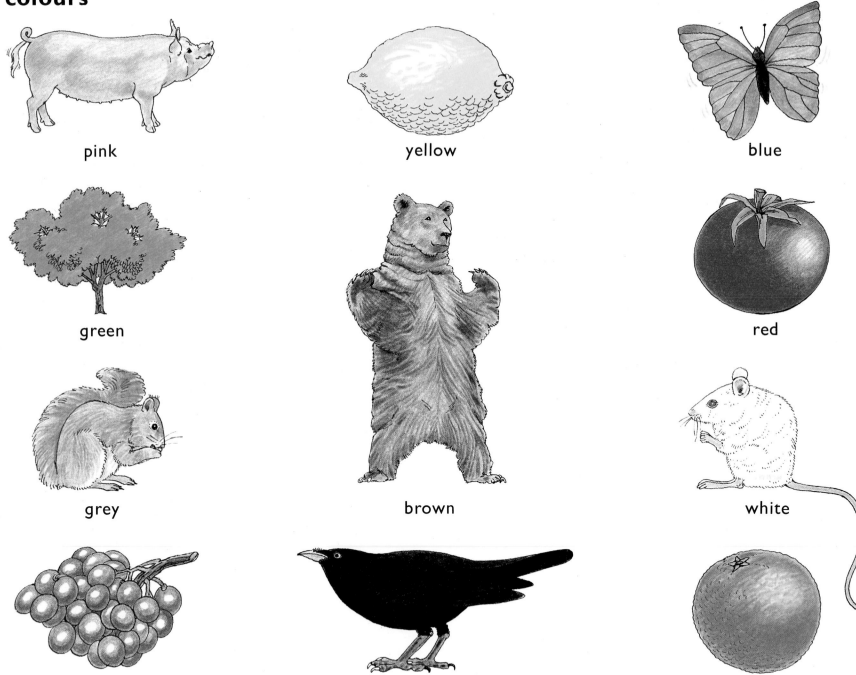

pink

yellow

blue

green

brown

red

grey

white

purple

black

orange

nought/zero

 one

 two

 three

 four

 five

 six

 seven

 eight

 nine

 ten

 eleven

 twelve

 thirteen

 fourteen

 fifteen

 sixteen

 seventeen

 eighteen

 nineteen

 twenty

 twenty-one

 thirty

 forty

 fifty

 sixty

 seventy

 eighty

 ninety

 a/one hundred

 a/one thousand

 a/one million

Index

Page numbers are printed in **thick** type. Numbers in plain type show where to find a word on the page. So 'chair 13/15' means that the word 'chair' is number 15 on page 13.

Aa across **45**/3
address **20**/8
aerial **10**/1
aeroplane **30**/6
air hostess **30**/7
airport **30**/8
alarm-clock **16**/9
ambulance **26**/9
animal **39**
ant **39**/8
apple **7**/1
April **49**
are **44**; **45**
armchair **14**/12
astronaut **1**/4
at **13**; **16**; **21**; **26**; **28**; **32**; **38**; **44**/6
athletics **35**/8
at the bottom of **44**/9
at the top of **44**/2
August **49**
aunt **24**/8
away **41**/1
axe **26**/14

Bb baby **8**/14
back **22**/10; **46**
bad **27**; **33**; **46**
bag **9**/11
ball **34**/6
balloon **21**/8; **30**/2
banana **7**/4
bandage **32**/13
bank **4**/9
baseball **34**/12
basin **18**/7
basket **5**/5
basketball **34**/11

bat **34**/14
bath **18**/14
bathmat **18**/10
bathroom **18**
beach **29**/10
bean **7**/11
bear **38**/10
beard **23**/4
beautiful **46**
bed **16**/2
bedroom **16**; **17**
bee **39**/1
beetle **39**/7
behind **44**/8
bell **26**/15
belt **27**/8
bicycle **20**/12
big **46**
bike **20**/12
bird **3**/12
birthday **21**
biscuit **21**/3
bite **43**/8
black **50**
blackboard **9**/4
blanket **16**/4
bleed **33**/10
blow **42**/15
blue **50**
blunt **46**
board-game **17**/14
boat **31**/11
body **22**
book **9**/7
bookcase **9**/6
bookstall **44**/6
boot **27**/14
bottle **5**/15
bottom **22**/11; **44**/9
bowl **13**/9
box **15**/10
boxing **35**/9
boy **8**/6
brake **20**/10
branch **11**/2
bread **5**/3

break **33**/2
brick **10**/7
bridge **8**/5; **45**/2, 6
brother **24**/5
brown **50**
brush **15**/13; **17**/10; **43**/1
bucket **28**/14
building **26**/6
bus **6**/10
bush **11**/5
bus-stop **6**/8
butcher **4**/12
butter **13**/11
butterfly **39**/2
button **19**/6
by **37**; **44**/1

Cc cabbage **7**/9
cage **38**/2
cake **21**/11
camel **38**/9
camera **21**/4
camp **33**/1
can **12**/5
candle **21**/10
canoe **28**/3
cap **27**/11
capsule **1**/15
captain **29**/14
car **37**/7
caravan **2**/12
card **21**/15
cardboard box **15**/10
car-park **4**/15
carpet **15**/12
carriage **17**/5
carrot **7**/12
carry **33**/5
cart **3**/2
cassette **40**/13
castle **17**/3
cat **39**/11
catch **36**/11
ceiling **15**/1
chair **13**/15
chalk **9**/3

check-out **5**/9
cheek **23**/12
cheese **12**/6
chemist **4**/7
chest **22**/3
chest of drawers **16**/15
chicken **3**/9
children **8**/7
chimney **10**/2
chin **23**/1
chocolate **8**/1
cinema **4**/3
circus **28**/1
clap **42**/5
classroom **9**
clean **41**/6; **46**
cliff **31**/4
climb **42**/7
clock **16**/9
closed **47**
clothes **25**
cloud **27**/3
coach **37**/4
coat **27**/9
coffee **5**/14
coffee-pot **12**/12
cold **47**
colour **50**
comb **16**/11; **43**/2
container-ship **29**/6
control-room **1**/14
cooker **12**/1
corner **6**/2
cotton **19**/5
country **2**; **45**/4, 5
court **34**/8
cousin **24**/9
cow **3**/11
crab **39**/15
crash-helmet **37**/5
crawl **43**/15
cricket **34**/13
crocodile **38**/4
crossing **6**/11
crossroads **6**/13
crowd **26**/10

cry **33/8**
cucumber **7/10**
cup **14/8**
cupboard **15/9**
curtain **16/8**
cushion **14/6**
customer **5/13**
cut **33/9**
cycling **35/3**

Dd daddy **24/3**
dance **42/11**
dark **47**
date **49**
daughter **24/13**
day **17**; **48**; **49**
December **49**
deck **31/13**
dentist **4/13**
desk **9/8**
dining-table **13/4**
dinosaur **44/3, 4**
dirty **46**
dive **36/1**
do **43**
doctor **32/6**
dog **8/8**
doll **21/6**
doll's house **19/8**
dolphin **38/8**
donkey **3/3**
door **10/9**; **44/1**
down **44/11**
downstairs **10/8**
draw **43/12**
drawer **16/14**
dream **43/3**
dress **25/7**
dressing-gown **16/1**
drink **28/5**; **43/7**
drive **36/12**
driver **37/9**
drum **40/5**
dry **47**
duck **3/15**
dustbin **10/11**

dustpan **15/14**

Ee eagle **38/1**
ear **23/15**
ear-ring **23/9**
earth **1/8**
easy **46**
egg **12/14**
eight **48**; **51**
eighteen **51**
eighty **51**
elbow **22/9**
electric mixer **12/15**
elephant **38/11**
eleven **51**
empty **46**
engine **30/9**; **37/8**; **45/11**
exercise-book **9/9**
eye **23/10**
eyebrow **23/2**

Ff face **22/2**
factory **4/2**
fair **28/2**
fall **33/3**
family **24**
farm **2/10**; **3**
farmer **3/4**
fast **46**
fat **46**
father **24/3**
February **49**
fence **3/8**; **11/7**
ferry **29/8**
field **2/9**
fifteen **51**
fifty **51**
finger **22/5**
fire **26**; **26/5**
fire-engine **26/8**
fire-escape **26/4**
fire-hose **26/13**
fireman **26/1**
fireplace **14/3**
fish **38/7**
fishing **35/7**

fishing-boat **29/1**
five **48**; **51**
flag **29/3**
flat **4/1**
floor **15/15**
flower **11/12**
flower-pot **11/13**
fly **36/5**; **39/3**
foot **22/14**
football **34/1**
footpath **10/12**
forest **2/4**
fork **11/14**; **13/3**
forty **51**
four **48**; **51**
fourteen **51**
freezer **5/6**
Friday **49**
fridge **12/7**
friend **21/1**
from **20**; **45/5**
front **44/4**; **46**
fruit **5/2**; **7**
frying-pan **12/8**
full **46**
fun **42**

Gg game **17/14**; **21/7**
garage **10/10**
garden **11**
gate **10/13**
girl **8/4**
give **42/13**
glass **13/14**
glasses **32/5**
glider **30/1**
glove **27/10**; **34/15**
glue **19/11**
go **45**
goal **34/2**
goat **3/7**
goggles **28/10**
good **46**
grandfather **24/1**
grandmother **24/2**
grape **7/3**

grass **11/10**
green **50**
grey **50**
grill **11/2**
group **40/7**
guitar **40/12**

Hh hair **23/6**
hairbrush **16/10**
hairdresser **4/11**
half **48**
hall **15**
hammer **19/15**
hand **22/1**; **42/8**
handbag **8/13**
handkerchief **32/4**
happy **46**
hard **46**
hat **27/6**
have **42**
head **22/8**; **23**
heavy **47**
hedge **3/13**
helicopter **30/11**; **31/2**
help **41**
hide **43/14**
high **47**
hill **2/5**
hit **36/14**
hole **31/14**
holiday **28**
horse **3/1**
hose **26/13**
hospital **32**
hot **47**
hotel **4/10**; **30/5**
hour **48**
house **10**
hug **42/12**
hundred **51**
husband **24/10**

Ii ice **8/10**
ice-cream **21/9**
in **2**; **4**; **5**; **6**; **7**; **8**; **9**; **12**; **17**; **30**; **44/4**

in front of **44**/7
injection **32**/7
inside **44**/4
into **1**; **45**/7
iron **19**/1; **41**/5
is **48**; **49**
island **31**/5
it **48**

Jj jacket **25**/9
jam **13**/12
January **49**
jeans **25**/10
jet engine **30**/9
jigsaw **17**/13
judo **35**/2
jug **13**/2
July **49**
jump **36**/6
June **49**

Kk keeper **38**/12
kettle **12**/10
key **37**/12
kick **36**/8
kiss **42**/2
kitchen **12**
kite **30**/4
knee **22**/12
knife **13**/10
knitting-needle **14**/4

Ll ladder **11**/4; **26**/3
lake **2**/2
lamp **14**/1
lamp-post **6**/6
land **29**/9
large **39**
laugh **42**/3
launch-pad **1**/12
lavatory **18**/1
lavatory-paper **18**/2
leaf **11**/3
left **47**
leg **22**/13; **44**/8
lemon **7**/7

letter **20**/1
letter-box **20**/6
lettuce **7**/8
lick **43**/9
lie **33**/6
lifeboat **29**/13
lift **32**/1
light **15**/3; **47**
lightning **27**/4
light-switch **15**/5
line **34**/3
liner **29**/4
lion **38**/6
lip **23**/13
listen **43**/13
little **46**
living-room **14**
long **47**
lorry **6**/3
low **47**
luck **33**
luggage **37**/13

Mm make **19**
man **8**/11
map **9**/1
March **49**
May **49**
meat **5**/7
medicine **32**/11
microphone **40**/8
midnight **48**
milk **12**/13; **20**/15
million **51**
minute **48**
mirror **18**/3
mixer **12**/15
Monday **49**
money **30**/14
monkey **38**/14
month **48**; **49**
moon **1**/6
moth **39**/5
mother **24**/4
motor-bike **37**/6
motor-boat **29**/12

motor-racing **35**/11
motorway **37**/2
mountain **2**/1
mouse **39**/10
moustache **23**/8
mouth **23**/5
mug **13**/1
mummy **24**/4
music **40**; **40**/14
my **22**; **23**

Nn nail **19**/14
name **20**/7
neck **23**/11
needle **14**/4
net **28**/7; **34**/9
new **47**
newspaper **32**/8
night **16**
nightie **16**/3
nine **51**
nineteen **51**
ninety **51**
noon **48**
nose **23**/7
nought **51**
November **49**
number **51**
number-plate **37**/14
nurse **32**/2
nut **7**/15

Oo o'clock **48**
October **49**
octopus **39**/14
off **45**/10
old **47**
on **3**; **29**; **44**/11
one **51**
onion **7**/14
onto **45**/9
open **41**/4; **47**
orange **7**/6; **50**
orbit **1**/7
out of **45**/8
outside **44**/5

oven **12**/3
over **45**/2

Pp paint **17**/11; **41**/3
pair **46**; **47**
pan **12**/9
panda **38**/15
pants **25**/5
paper **17**/12
parachute **30**/3
parcel **20**/5
park **8**
party **21**
pass **36**/13
passenger **30**/15
past **45**/11; **48**
path **2**/11
patient **32**/10
pavement **6**/15
pear **7**/2
pedestrian crossing **6**/11
pen **9**/14
pencil **9**/13
penguin **38**/13
penknife **19**/10
pepper **13**/7
petrol-pump **6**/5
petrol-station **6**/4
photograph **32**/9
piano **40**/10
pick up **33**/7
picnic **28**/6
picture **15**/4
pig **3**/14
pill **32**/12
pillow **16**/7
pilot **31**/3
pin **19**/2
pineapple **7**/5
pink **50**
pipe **10**/6
planet **1**/10
plant **15**/6; **41**/10
plaster **32**/15
plate **13**/5
platform **17**/6; **45**/9

play 42/10
player 34/5; 40/2
playground 4/8
pocket 25/11
police-car 26/11
policeman 26/12
police-station 6/1
pond 2/15
pop group 40/7
porter 45/12
post 43/10
post-box 20/6
postcard 20/4
poster 17/1
postman 20/2
post office 4/6; 20
pot 11/13
potato 7/13
pour 41/2
pram 8/15
present 21/2
puddle 27/15
pull 41/13
pump 20/11
pupil 9/5
puppet 21/5
purple 50
purse 5/11
push 41/11
put away 41/1
pyjamas 16/6

Qq quarter 48

Rr rabbit 3/10
racket 34/10
radio 14/15
raft 29/11
railway 45/3
rain 27/5
rainbow 27/1
raincoat 27/13
read 43/11
record 21/13; 40/15
recorder 40/4
record-player 21/14

red 50
rescue 31
restaurant 4/5
ride 36/4
right 47
ring 28/8
river 2/7
road 6/9; 37
rock 31/15
rocket 1/1
roof 10/3
rope 31/6
rope-ladder 11/4
round 45/12
roundabout 37/3
rowing 35/15
rowing-boat 29/7
rubber 9/12
rug 16/13
rugby 35/6
ruler 9/10
run 36/15
runway 30/12

Ss sad 46
sail 31/9; 36/2
sailor 31/7
salt 13/6
sand 28/15
satchel 9/15
satellite 1/9
Saturday 49
saucer 14/9
saw 19/9
scales 18/9
scarf 8/3
school 4/10
scissors 19/4
screw 19/12
screwdriver 19/13
sea 29; 31/10
seaside 28
seat 37/11
seat-belt 37/10
see-saw 11/8
second 48

September 49
seven 48; 51
seventeen 51
seventy 51
sew 41/9
sewing-machine 19/3
shake (hands) 42/8
shampoo 18/13
shark 39/13
sharp 46
shed 10/15
sheep 3/6
sheet 16/5
shelf 5/4
shell 28/4
ship 31/8
shirt 25/15
shoe 25/14
shoelace 25/13
shoot 36/7
shop 4/14
short 47
shorts 25/6
shout 42/6
shower 18/11
shut 41/15; 47
signpost 37/1
sing 42/9
singer 40/6
sink 12/11
sister 24/6
sit 33/12
six 48; 51
sixteen 51
sixty 51
skating 35/1
ski-ing 35/12
skirt 25/12
sky 27/2; 30
sleep 43/4
slice 21/12
slide 11/9
slipper 16/12
slow 46
small 39
smile 42/14

smoke 26/2
snake 38/5
snow 8/9
snowman 8/2
soap 18/12
sock 25/3
sofa 14/5
soldier 17/15
son 24/12
space 1
space-shuttle 1/2
space-station 1/13
space-suit 1/5
spade 11/15; 28/13
spider 39/6
sponge 18/15
spoon 13/8
sport 34; 35; 36
staircase 15/8
stairs 44/2, 9
stamp 20/9
stand 33/4
star 1/11
station 17/7; 45/7, 8
sting 33/15
stir 41/3
stool 14/14; 40/11
storm 31/1
stream 2/14
street 6
stretcher 32/14
string 20/3; 40/9
strong 47
submarine 29/7
suitcase 37/15
sun 1/3
Sunday 49
sun-glasses 28/9
supermarket 5
sweater 25/8
sweep 41/14
sweets 5/10
swim 36/10
swimming 35/4
swimming-costume 28/11
swimming-pool 35/5

swimming-trunks **28**/12
swing **11**/6; **42**/4
switch **15**/5

Tt T-shirt **25**/1
table **13**/4
table tennis **35**/10
tail **44**/7
tanker **29**/2
tap **18**/5
tea **5**/12
teacher **9**/2
team **34**/4
teapot **14**/7
tear **33**/13
telephone **15**/7
telephone-box **6**/7
television **14**/2
ten **48**; **51**
tennis **34**/7
tent **2**/13
they **45**
thin **46**
thing **19**; **43**
thirteen **51**
thirty **51**
thousand **51**
three **48**; **51**
through **45**/1
throw **36**/9
thumb **22**/6
Thursday **49**
ticket **30**/13

tie **33**/14
tiger **38**/3
time **48**; **49**
to **31**; **45**/4; **48**
toast **13**/13
toe **22**/15
toilet **18**/1
toilet-paper **18**/2
tongue **23**/3
tooth **23**/14
toothbrush **18**/4
toothpaste **18**/6
top **44**/2
torch **17**/9
towel **18**/8
town **4**
toys **17**/2
track suit **35**/15
tractor **3**/5
traffic-light **6**/12
train **17**/8; **45**/10
trainers **35**/14
tray **14**/10
tree **11**/1
trolley **5**/8
trousers **25**/2
truck **17**/4
trumpet **40**/1
T-shirt **25**/1
Tuesday **49**
tug **29**/5
tummy **22**/4
tunnel **45**/1

turn **41**/17
twelve **51**
twenty **48**; **51**
twenty-one **51**
two **51**
tyre **20**/14

Uu ugly **46**
umbrella **27**/12
uncle **24**/7
under **45**/6
up **44**/10
upstairs **10**/4

Vv vacuum-cleaner **15**/11
valley **2**/3
van **6**/14
vegetables **5**/1; **7**
vest **25**/4
village **2**/6
violin **40**/3

Ww wake **43**/5
walk **36**/3
wall **15**/2
wash **41**/8
washing-line **10**/14
washing-machine **12**/4
wasp **39**/4
waste-paper basket **14**/11
watch **32**/3
water **26**/7
wave **31**/12; **42**/1

we **44**
weak **47**
weather **27**
Wednesday **49**
week **48**; **49**
wet **47**
whale **39**/12
what **48**; **49**
wheel **20**/13
wheel-barrow **11**/11
where **44**; **45**
white **50**
wife **24**/11
wind **27**/7
window **10**/5; **44**/5
wing **30**/10
woman **8**/12
wood **2**/8
wool **14**/13
world **1**/8
worm **39**/9
write **33**/11

Xx

Yy year **48**
yellow **50**
young **47**

Zz zero **51**
zip **19**/7
zoo **38**